TOP 10 WOMEN'S BASKETBALL STARS

Jeff Savage

SPORTS TOP 10

Enslow Publishers, Inc.

40 Industrial Road   PO Box 38
Box 398   Aldershot
Berkeley Heights, NJ 07922   Hants GU12 6BP
USA   UK

http://www.enslow.com

Library of Congress Cataloging-in-Publication Data

Savage, Jeff, 1961–
    Top 10 women's basketball stars / Jeff Savage.
        p. cm. — (Sports top 10)
    Includes bibliographical references and index.
    ISBN 0-7660-1496-7
    1. Basketball players—Unites States—Biography—Juvenile literature.
    2. Women basketball players—United States—Biography—Juvenile literature.
    3. Women basketball players—Rating of—United States—Juvenile literature.
    [1. Basketball players. 2. Women—Biography.] I. Title: Top ten women's
basketball stars. II. Title. III. Series.
GV884.A1 S296   2001
796.323'082'092273—dc21

                                     00-009525

Printed in the United States of America

10 9 8 7 6 5 4 3 2 1

To Our Readers: All Internet addresses in this book were active and appropriate
when we went to press. Any comments or suggestions can be sent by e-mail to
Comments@enslow.com or to the address on the back cover.

Illustration Credits: Allen Einstein/NBA Photos, p. 25; Barry Gossage/NBA
Photos, pp. 21, 37, 39; Basketball Hall of Fame, Springfield, Mass., pp. 11, 31;
Bill Baptist/NBA Photos, pp. 7, 9, 23, 33, 41, 45; Charles Smith, Jr./NBA Photos,
p. 29; David Liam/NBA Photos, p. 17; Fernando Medina/NBA Photos, p. 42;
Greg Shamus/NBA Photos, p. 26; Mitchell Layton/NBA Photos, p. 15; Old
Dominion University, p. 13; Peter Read Miller/NBA Photos, p. 35; Robert
Mora/NBA Photos, p. 19.

Cover Illustration: Bill Baptist/NBA Photos.

Cover Description: Cynthia Cooper of the Houston Comets.

Interior Design: Richard Stalzer

CONTENTS

INTRODUCTION

"WE GOT NEXT!" That slogan has marked the movement of women's basketball to the forefront of professional sports. Some slogans are pure hype, but "We got next!," which means we have the next game on the court, rings true. With the birth of the Women's National Basketball Association (WNBA) in 1997, and a rising interest in the college game, women's basketball in the United States has blossomed. From the excitement a whole new cast of sports stars has emerged. Rebecca Lobo, Lisa Leslie, Sheryl Swoopes, Cynthia Cooper, Chamique Holdsclaw, and Dawn Staley have become household names. But as Staley says, "The great players and the game have always been there. They just haven't gotten the same level of coverage."[1]

Indeed, the women's game started in 1892, less than a year after Dr. James Naismith invented it for men. Senda Berenson adapted it for her physical education classes at Smith College as a form of exercise. But the rules for girls were different. Only one player on each team could play full court. A player had to pass or shoot after three dribbles. Men were not permitted to watch games, and the women in attendance were told to keep silent because cheering was considered unladylike.

Eventually the rules for girls changed to make the game more like we now know it, and a whole generation of female athletes arose. Among the pioneers was Ann Meyers, who is known as basketball's "Lady of Firsts" for her long list of accomplishments. Next were Anne Donovan and Nancy Lieberman-Cline, whose Olympic achievements gave the United States worldwide recognition in the sport. Then came Cheryl Miller, whose acrobatic moves raised the level of play. Finally, after a string of professional leagues failed, the WNBA has provided a stage for a band of new stars.

A great basketball player is made up of many qualities. She has the gritty determination that Dawn Staley exemplifies when she raps her knuckles to the hardwood. She has the dedication of Rebecca Lobo, who might not be the greatest athlete, but whose hustle and heart translated to 105 straight victories stretching three years. Lobo's style of play and court presence provide a flair not unlike that of Lisa Leslie and Sheryl Swoopes and others who weave their magic on the court. Choosing the top ten women's basketball players was not easy. With so many stars emerging in a sport that is just now taking hold, it is difficult to say who is the best. The ten we have selected certainly stand out, but there are others who would make someone's top ten list. Here is *our* list.

CAREER STATISTICS (WNBA)

Player	Team	Years	RPG	APG	FT%	PTS	PPG
ƴNTHIA COOPER	HOUSTON	1997–1999	3.5	4.8	.869	1,987	22.3
ᴎNE DONOVAN	OLD DOMINION*	1980–1983	14.5	2.0	.661	2,719	20.0
ᴴAMIQUE HOLDSCLAW	WASHINGTON	1999	7.9	2.4	.773	525	16.9
ISA LESLIE	LOS ANGELES	1997–1999	9.1	2.3	.695	1,494	17.0
ᴵANCY LIEBERMAN-CLINE	OLD DOMINION*	1977–1980	8.7	7.2	.757	2,430	18.1
ᴱBECCA LOBO	NEW YORK	1997–1999	7.0	1.6	.657	698	11.8
ᴎNN MEYERS	UCLA*	1975–1978	8.4	5.6	.785	1,685	17.4
ᴴERYL MILLER	USC*	1983–1986	12.0	3.2	.735	3,018	23.7
ᴰAWN STALEY	CHARLOTTE	1999	2.3	5.5	.934	368	11.5
HERYL SWOOPES	HOUSTON	1997–1999	5.2	2.8	.815	1,102	15.7

ᴿPG=REBOUNDS PER GAME   **APG**=ASSISTS PER GAME   **FT%**=FREE-THROW PERCENTAGE
TS=POINTS   **PPG**=POINTS PER GAME

College statistics are listed for those who had their greatest success prior to the formation of
ᴛe WNBA.

ll stats are through the 1999 season.

CYNTHIA COOPER

THE FINAL BUZZER SOUNDED, and the confetti fell to the court. The Houston Comets had won the 1999 WNBA title, and Cynthia Cooper finally could celebrate.

Three weeks earlier, Comets point guard Kim Perrot had died of cancer. Cooper dedicated the rest of the season to Perrot's memory and all but guaranteed a third straight championship for the Comets. It almost did not work out that way. The New York Liberty scored on a fifty-foot prayer at the buzzer to steal Game 2 of the finals from the Comets and force a deciding third game. This time, Cooper took control. She scored 24 points to lead her team to a 59–47 triumph. "The person that we didn't stop was Cooper," said New York coach Richie Adubato. "Cooper proved what a great player she was."[1] Cooper had good reason to dance on the scorer's table at the Compaq Center in Houston, waving Perrot's jersey over her head and then putting it on over her own jersey. "After all we've been through as a team, it feels great to 'threepeat,'" said Cooper. "It's been extremely tough."[2]

Cynthia Cooper is no stranger to tragedy. She was born April 14, 1963, in Chicago, Illinois, the youngest of eight children raised by Mary Cobb, a single mother. Cynthia grew up in Watts, a poor section of Los Angeles, California. Once, her house burned down in an electrical fire. "We lost everything," Cynthia said. "And we didn't have anything to lose."[3] Cynthia persevered as a confident and athletic child. "As a kid I played detective with my friends," she said. "I was Sherlock Holmes because I wanted to be the leader."[4] At Locke High School in Los Angeles she ran track, and broke the city record in the 300-meter hurdles. She did not

Leaping into the air, Cynthia Cooper goes up for the layup. Cooper played in Europe for many years before she joined the newly-formed WNBA in 1997.

join the school basketball team until age sixteen, after being inspired by seeing another girl put the ball behind her back and make a layup. Cooper averaged 8 points as a junior, then worked extremely hard on her game, and raised her average to 31 points per game as a senior.

Cooper was awarded a scholarship to the University of Southern California (USC) where she and teammate Cheryl Miller led the Trojans to back-to-back national championships. While Cooper was at USC, her brother Everett was stabbed in a street fight. She was at the hospital when he died on the operating table. Her brother's death so overwhelmed her that she left school to work at a bank. A year later, USC coach Linda Sharp convinced her to return to USC to play basketball her senior year. After college, she played professionally in Spain and Italy over the next eleven years. She also played often for the U.S. national team, winning a handful of medals, including Olympic gold in 1988.

In 1996, Cooper was playing for a team in Parma, Italy, when she heard about the newly forming WNBA. She called Renee Brown, the director of player personnel. "I said, 'My name's Cynthia Cooper and I play in Italy,'" said Cooper. "She was like, 'Cynthia Cooper? Italy? You play in Parma, right? Oh, girl, you're in our top 16! Where do we send the contract?'"[5]

Two months before Cooper debuted with the Houston Comets, her mother was diagnosed with cancer. As Mary Cobbs underwent treatment, Cooper led the league in scoring while carrying the Comets to the 1997 WNBA title. Cooper repeated the feat in 1998. In February 1999, Cooper's mother died of cancer. Two weeks later, Kim Perrot was diagnosed with the disease. Cooper overcame the tragedies to lead her team to a third straight title. "You get slapped in the face, you get knocked down," said Cooper, "you just get up tougher than before."[6]

CYNTHIA COOPER

BORN: April 14, 1963, Chicago, Illinois.

HIGH SCHOOL: Locke High School, Los Angeles, California.

COLLEGE: University of Southern California.

PRO: European League, 1986–1996; Houston Comets, 1997– .

RECORDS: WNBA scoring champion, 1997–1999; WNBA three-point scoring leader; WNBA all-time scoring leader.

HONORS: Member of NCAA national championship team, 1983–1984; European All-Star Game MVP, 1987; Olympic gold medalist, 1988; WNBA MVP, 1997–1998; WNBA Championship Series MVP, 1997–1999.

Cooper splits two Sacramento Monarchs defenders to make room for her shot.

Cynthia Cooper
http://www.wnba.com/playerfile/cynthia_cooper.html

ANNE DONOVAN

ANNE DONOVAN SAT ON THE BENCH, wondering if she would ever get another chance. She was playing on her third and final Olympic team. But at the 1988 Olympic Games in Seoul, Korea, she was getting on the court for only about three minutes a game. At six feet eight inches, Donovan was the tallest player on the U.S. team, and coach Kay Yow had decided to go with quickness over height. In four previous games, Donovan, the team's captain, had scored a total of one basket.

Donovan watched helplessly as her team struggled against Yugoslavia in the title game. The Americans could not stop mighty Yugoslav center Razija Mujanovic. Finally, with 4:04 remaining in the first half, and the United States trailing 32–30, coach Yow called on Donovan. Could the veteran center help?

Donovan seized the moment. Seventeen seconds after checking in, she drilled a 17-footer from straightaway to tie it up. Next she batted away an entry pass to Mujanovic that led to a fast break basket by Bridgette Gordon for a 34–32 United States lead. Then she knocked away another inside pass, got fouled at the other end, and made both free throws for a 36–32 lead. After the teams traded baskets, she blocked Mujanovic's shot, then nailed a baseline jumper to make it 40–34. Donovan had single-handedly turned the game around. She started the second half and finished with 6 points, 3 rebounds, 3 blocks, and more important, an Olympic gold medal. After the 77–70 victory, coach Yow said, "A lot of credit for this goes to Anne Donovan. The character Anne Donovan showed as a person is important.

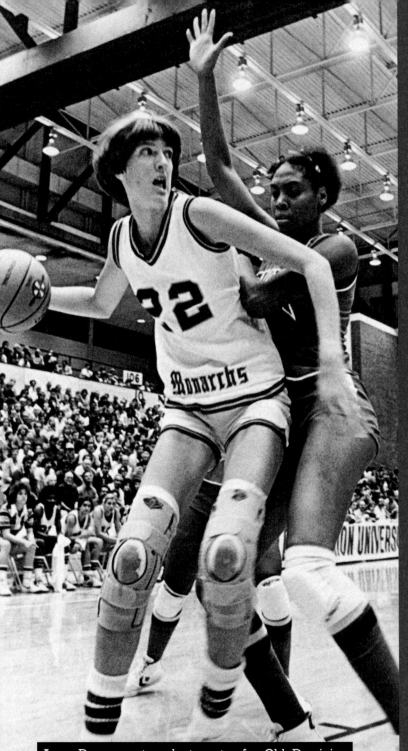

ANNE DONOVAN

Anne Donovan starred at center for Old Dominion University and then for USA Basketball throughout the 1980s. In 2000, she became head coach of the expansion Indiana Fever of the WNBA.

She didn't start, she didn't play real well in the tournament, yet she maintained a great positive attitude. And she made the difference today."[1]

Anne Donovan was born November 1, 1961, in Ridgewood, New Jersey. By the sixth grade she was six feet tall and towered over her opponents. She led Paramus (New Jersey) Catholic High School to an undefeated season and a state championship in both her junior and senior years. She averaged 35 points and 17 rebounds a game her final season and was an easy choice for National Player of the Year.

As the most highly recruited teenager in the country, Donovan chose Old Dominion University in Virginia. As a six-foot six-inch freshman she was quick on her feet, and she swatted away anything that was put up from in close. By her senior year, she had grown two more inches, and had led the nation in blocked shots all four years. She still owns the National Collegiate Athletic Association (NCAA) women's record with 801 career blocks. She blocked 15 shots in a single game, scored 50 points in another, and pulled down 10 or more rebounds in 114 games. Her inside dominance meant success for the Lady Monarchs who went an amazing 37–1 on their way to the national championship her freshman year. Though Old Dominion did not win the title again with Donovan, it did compile a brilliant 116–20 record to establish itself as a solid women's basketball program.

When Donovan was not setting college records, she was collecting medals. Starting in 1978 with a gold medal at the Olympic Festival, Donovan was a member of twelve U.S. National Teams that won nine gold medals and two silvers. She played professionally for five years in Japan and another in Europe, before returning to America to coach. She coached at East Carolina University, and later with the Philadelphia Rage of the ABL, giving younger players someone to look up to.

ANNE DONOVAN

BORN: November 1, 1961, Ridgewood, New Jersey.

HIGH SCHOOL: Paramus Catholic High School, Paramus, New Jersey.

COLLEGE: Old Dominion University.

PRO: Japan League, 1983–1988; European League, 1988–1989.

RECORDS: Led NCAA in blocked shots in a season, 1980–1983; holds NCAA record for career blocked shots, 1980–1983.

HONORS: National High School Player of the Year, 1979; NCAA All-America, 1981–1983; NCAA Player of the Year, 1983; Olympic gold medalist, 1984, 1988; elected to Naismith Memorial Basketball Hall of Fame, 1995.

Donovan played overseas in women's pro leagues for six years before returning to America to begin her coaching career.

Anne Donovan
http://www.wnba.com/fever/coach.html

CHAMIQUE HOLDSCLAW

IT WAS AN ANNIVERSARY for the University of Tennessee. Chamique Holdsclaw wanted to celebrate it with a victory party. On March 29, 1987, the Lady Vols had won their first national basketball championship. Now exactly eleven years later, the Lady Vols were in the NCAA Championship Game once again. In addition, their opponent was Louisiana Tech, just as it had been eleven years earlier. Would history repeat itself?

Holdsclaw made it happen. She came out firing, first with a pair of driving layups, next with a jumper over the top. When the defense rotated toward her, she dished the ball off to Tamika Catchings and Kellie Jolly for easy baskets. With seven minutes left in the first half, the Volunteers had built a commanding 42–17 lead. Louisiana Tech could not stop Holdsclaw. She finished with 25 points, 10 rebounds, and 6 assists, as the Lady Vols coasted to a 93–75 victory. Afterward, Holdsclaw was thrilled but calm, living up to her nickname "Meek." But then, winning championships was nothing new to her. This was the eighth year in a row she had led her team to a title.

Chamique Holdsclaw was born August 9, 1977, in Flushing, New York. She was raised mostly by her grandmother, June Holdsclaw, who instilled religion and confidence in her. Chamique studied hard in school, but her first love was basketball. "I knew I wasn't going to be average," she said.[1] Her grandmother knew it too. "In eighth grade, she could throw the ball all the way from one end of the court to the other," said June Holdsclaw. "And she was so skinny!"[2] That same eighth-grade year, Chamique began

Chamique Holdsclaw shoots a jumper over Eva Nemcova of the Cleveland Rockers. At the University of Tennessee, Holdsclaw led the Lady Volunteers to three national titles.

her streak of titles by winning the Queens Lutheran School Eighth Grade Championship.

Chamique Holdsclaw dominated New York City high school basketball like nobody before her. She led her Christ the King High School team to four state championships and a national title with an overall record of 106–4. She was the first player, male or female, to be named New York City Player of the Year three straight years. She was also New York State's Most Valuable Player three times, and the National Player of the Year in 1995. She had become so popular that she wrote a weekly diary for *USA Today*.

Now people were calling Holdsclaw the best woman basketball player ever, even better than the great Cheryl Miller. "When I recruited her," said Tennessee coach Pat Summit, "I kept mentioning Cheryl Miller. She kept telling me, 'I don't want to be Cheryl Miller. I want to be Chamique Holdsclaw.'"[3]

At Tennessee, Holdsclaw's quickness and many moves made her unstoppable. She wore Michael Jordan's number, twenty-three, and her spin moves and fadeaway jumpers drew comparisons to the NBA great. In her four college years, she set a near endless list of team, conference, and national records. Among her many achievements was being the first collegiate woman ever to receive the prestigious Sullivan Award, given to the nation's top amateur athlete.

Holdsclaw was an easy choice as the top pick in the 1999 WNBA draft, and she starred at forward for the Washington Mystics, averaging nearly 17 points and 9 rebounds per game her rookie year. One month into the season, "Meek" had already become a fan favorite, being voted by fans as a starter for the inaugural WNBA All-Star Game. She suffered a broken finger in the game on a tipped pass. Three days later, with her broken finger bandaged, she was back on the court in her Mystics uniform ready to play.

BORN: August 9, 1977, Flushing, New York.

HIGH SCHOOL: Christ the King High School, Astoria, New York.

COLLEGE: University of Tennessee.

PRO: Washington Mystics, 1999– .

RECORDS: Southeastern Conference all-time leading scorer, 1996–1999; NCAA Tournament career leading scorer and rebounder, 1996–1999.

HONORS: High school All-America, 1992–1995; member of NCAA national championship team, 1996–1998; NCAA All-America, 1996–1999; NCAA Player of the Year, 1998–1999; first college woman to win Sullivan Award (outstanding amateur athlete), 1999.

Putting the ball on the floor, Holdsclaw tries to make a move to get past her defender.

Chamique Holdsclaw
http://www.wnba.com/playerfile/chamique_holdsclaw.html

LISA LESLIE

LISA LESLIE LOOKED UP at the pinwheel ceiling and realized her situation. She was warming up on the floor of famous Madison Square Garden in New York City, surrounded by a sellout crowd of nearly nineteen thousand fans. The event was the 1999 WNBA All-Star Game, the first ever staged, and Leslie decided to put on a show.

With superstars like Sheryl Swoopes and Cynthia Cooper stretching and practicing jump shots around her, Leslie did something fancy. She dribbled a basketball down the lane, soared high through the air, and slammed it home. A chorus of ooohs and aaahs rang out at the sight of a woman slam dunking. Unfortunately, Leslie's Western Conference teammates did not see it. "It was a good one," Leslie said with a smile. "I was pretty surprised no one noticed because they weren't paying attention."[1]

The other players certainly noticed Leslie in the game. Although she did not dunk the ball, she dominated inside the paint. She blocked shots, grabbed rebounds, and scored 13 points to lead her team to an easy 79–61 victory. Leslie was named the All-Star Game Most Valuable Player. "I feel really honored to have this award," she said.[2]

Even before Lisa Leslie grew to be six feet five inches, she often stood out from the crowd. She was born July 7, 1972, in Southern California. When she was two years old, her father left home. Her mother, Christine, took a job as a mail carrier, and when Lisa was nine, her mother became a long-haul truck driver to earn more money. In the summertime, Lisa and her sisters, Dionne and Tiffany, got to go on cross-country trips, eat at roadside diners, and sleep

LISA LESLIE

Lisa Leslie of the Los Angeles Sparks beats the defense down the court. Leslie keeps busy off the court as well, having done some acting and modeling.

overnight in the cab of their mother's truck. During the school year, her mother was gone for month-long stretches, so Lisa and her sisters were raised by an aunt. Lisa sometimes held a framed picture of her mother in bed and cried herself to sleep.

By the seventh grade, Leslie was already six feet tall. Her classmates teasingly called her Olive Oyl, after the character in *Popeye* cartoons. Her mother told her not to stoop, and to be proud of her height. She had avoided playing basketball until then because she was *expected* to play, but a friend convinced her to try it, and so she joined the seventh-grade girls team. She enjoyed the action so much that a year later she joined an all-boys league in Los Angeles called Slam-n-Jam.

Lisa Leslie blossomed into a star player at Morningside High, where she led her team to two state championships. In one game she scored 101 points—in the first half! She did not get a chance to add to the total because the opposing team forfeited the game at halftime. She was offered dozens of college scholarships, and she chose nearby USC, where in 1994 she was the National Player of the Year. Two years later, she led the United States to the Olympic gold medal, scoring 29 points against Brazil in the title game.

Leslie soon became a media sensation. She appeared on magazine covers and television talk shows and signed a contract with a modeling agency. A year later she signed another contract—this one with her hometown Los Angeles Sparks of the WNBA. Leslie is the first to admit she becomes a different person when she steps on a basketball court. "It's like this Wonder Woman thing," she says. "I'm the most polite person you'll ever meet off the court. But I put on my uniform and . . . what can I say? My hair's a mess. I'm yelling. I don't care. Don't mess with my teammates, don't mess with me. I want to win."[3]

LISA LESLIE

BORN: July 7, 1972, Gardena, California.

HIGH SCHOOL: Morningside High School, Inglewood, California.

COLLEGE: University of Southern California.

PRO: European League, 1994–1995; Los Angeles Sparks, 1997– .

RECORDS: Pacific-10 Conference all-time leading scorer, rebounder, and shot blocker; WNBA all-time leading rebounder.

HONORS: USA Basketball Athlete of the Year, 1993, 1998; NCAA All-America, 1993–1994; NCAA Player of the Year, 1994; Olympic gold medalist, 1996; WNBA All-Star MVP, 1999.

Awaiting the rebound, Leslie boxes out her opponent.

Lisa Leslie
http://www.wnba.com/playerfile/lisa_leslie.html

NANCY LIEBERMAN-CLINE

NEARLY ONE HUNDRED FIFTY WOMEN were at the regional tryout for the 1974 USA Women's National Basketball Team. The top ten would advance to the national tryouts in Albuquerque, New Mexico. Nancy Lieberman stepped onto the hardwood floor with the others as the youngest in the group, just fifteen years old.

Lieberman and the others were put through exhaustive drills. Her sneakers squeaked and her red hair bounced wildly as she kept up with the women. When the competition was over, the names of the ten finalists were posted on a board. Lieberman's name was on the list. "I was so excited," she said. "I called home and said, 'Mom! Mom! Guess what? I'm going to Albuquerque!'"[1]

Nancy Lieberman-Cline was born July 1, 1958, in Brooklyn, New York. She was never particularly tall for her age, although her full-grown height is five feet ten inches. When she was ten, she was a starter on a local YMCA boys team. By age thirteen, she was taking the train to Harlem each day to play against New York's best. She would challenge anyone to a game. People thought she was crazy. "But they saw I could play, that I wasn't afraid, and they respected that," said Lieberman. "They called me 'Fire' because of my red hair. It got to where I could walk through Harlem, and people would call out, 'Hey, Fire!' It was such a neat feeling. It wasn't about a white girl being in a black neighborhood; it was about people respecting people."[2]

Soon after Lieberman's tryouts in Albuquerque, she was with Team USA on a trip to Bogotá, Colombia, where she won a gold medal in the Pan American Games. At the 1976

Despite being much older than many of her teammates, Nancy Lieberman-Cline played for the Phoenix Mercury of the WNBA. She had been inducted into the Hall of Fame a year earlier.

Olympics in Montreal, Canada, Lieberman had just turned eighteen when she showed the world her feistiness. The giant Russian center, seven-foot two-inch, 280-pound Uljana Semjonova, came barreling down the lane. Lieberman stood her ground and courageously took a charge. The U.S. team won the silver, and Lieberman became the youngest basketball player in history to win an Olympic medal.

Nancy Lieberman set numerous collegiate records while leading Old Dominion University to a 72–2 record and back-to-back national titles in 1979 and 1980. She was chosen as the top draft pick by the Dallas Diamonds of the Women's Basketball League (WBL). In 1981, she became the personal trainer for tennis star Martina Navratilova. Three years later she rejoined the resurrected Dallas Diamonds in a new league, the Women's American Basketball Association (WABA), and led them to the league title.

Lieberman became the first woman ever to play in a men's professional league when she joined the United States Basketball League's Springfield Fame for the 1986 season. A year later she joined the Washington Generals—the team that plays against the famous traveling-comedy-act Harlem Globetrotters. The following year she married Tim Cline, another Generals player.

Lieberman-Cline went on to become a television sports broadcaster, a successful businesswoman, and a spokesperson for such organizations as the Special Olympics and Juvenile Diabetes. In May 1996 she was inducted into the Naismith Memorial Basketball Hall of Fame. A year later, at age thirty-nine, she was playing again. She came out of retirement to play in the inaugural WNBA season as a member of the Phoenix Mercury. "I wanted to show myself that I can still play the game at this level," said Lieberman-Cline. "I have nothing to prove. I want to do this."[3] A year later she became coach and general manager of the Detroit Shock.

NANCY LIEBERMAN-CLINE

BORN: July 1, 1958, Brooklyn, New York.

HIGH SCHOOL: Far Rockaway High School, Far Rockaway, New York.

COLLEGE: Old Dominion University.

PRO: Dallas Diamonds, 1980, 1984; Springfield Fame, 1986–1987; Phoenix Mercury, 1997; Detroit Shock (coach), 1998– .

RECORDS: Youngest Olympic basketball player ever to win a medal, 1976; set numerous Old Dominion records, including career assists and steals.

HONORS: High School All-America, 1974–1976; member of NCAA national championship team, 1979–1980; NCAA All-America, 1978–1980; NCAA Player of the Year, 1979–1980; elected to Naismith Memorial Basketball Hall of Fame, 1996.

After hanging up her sneakers for the last time, Lieberman-Cline accepted the head coaching position for the Detroit Shock.

Nancy Lieberman-Cline
http://www.wnba.com/shock/coach.html

REBECCA LOBO

Posting up her defender, Rebecca Lobo begins to make her way toward the basket.

REBECCA LOBO

THE FANS HAD GONE HOME. Gampel Pavilion at the University of Connecticut was quiet now except for the clean-up crew in the stands. Rebecca Lobo emerged from the locker room to greet her parents on the court. Lobo had scored 20 points to lead the Huskies to a win over the University of Virginia. "I'd had a great night," said Lobo. "I was having the best basketball week of my life."[1]

Rebecca's mother, Ruth Ann, took her aside and sat her down. Rebecca knew something was terribly wrong. Ruth Ann had been diagnosed with cancer. "Now, don't cry," Rebecca's mother told her. "You take care of basketball, and I'll take care of my health."[2]

After that, Lobo played basketball like never before. She led the Huskies to a 27–2 record and a tournament berth in 1994, followed by a perfect 35–0 season and NCAA Title in 1995. Meanwhile, her mother underwent surgery and seven months of treatment and is free of cancer. Their story is one of courage and love.

Rebecca Lobo was born October 6, 1973, in Hartford, Connecticut. When she was two, she moved with her family to Southwick, Massachusetts. One day, Rebecca joined her older brother, Jason, in a game of basketball on the family driveway. She fell in love with the game, and even used it to deal with childhood problems. "Many people, particularly young kids, need some way to handle the pain or anxiety, no matter how small or profound, in their lives. Basketball became my way," she said.[3]

Lobo's parents encouraged her love of sports. But others did not see things the same way. Her fifth-grade teacher called her to the front of class one day to tell her to change her ways. "She told me I was too much of a tomboy," said Lobo, "and that I needed to dress and act more like a girl."[4] But Rebecca's parents insisted that their daughter's happiness was what mattered, not an old-fashioned image. "We taught our children that everyone has his or her own gifts, talents, and worth," said Ruth Ann Lobo. "There is nothing wrong with a girl playing sports and wearing jeans."[5]

Rebecca Lobo scored 32 points in her first varsity game at Southwick Tolland Regional High School and averaged nearly that many (29.8) thereafter. Her Rams won four straight county titles and two Western Massachusetts state titles. She excelled academically as well and enrolled at Connecticut where she led the Huskies to the NCAA Tournament all four years—finally winning it all her senior year. Lobo joined the U.S. National Team on a fifty-two-game world tour to prepare for the Olympics. Lobo's team won every game. After beating Brazil in the Olympic final to win the gold medal, Lobo had won 95 straight games. By now she was a national celebrity who appeared on talk shows, and even went jogging with President Clinton.

In 1997, Lobo joined the WNBA's New York Liberty. The Liberty won its first seven contests, extending Lobo's winning streak to 102 games. On July 7, the Phoenix Mercury snapped the streak. It was Lobo's first loss in three years. She got revenge against the Mercury in the playoff semifinal with 16 points, 9 rebounds, 4 assists, and 3 blocks to lead her team to the inaugural WNBA title game. Though the Liberty lost to the streaking Houston Comets, Lobo remains a fan favorite. She suffered a torn knee ligament one minute into the 1999 season and missed the entire year. Even though she could not play, the fans still voted for her as a starter for the league's All-Star Game.

REBECCA LOBO

BORN: October 6, 1973, Hartford, Connecticut.

HIGH SCHOOL: Southwick Tolland Regional High School, Southwick, Massachusetts.

COLLEGE: University of Connecticut.

PRO: New York Liberty, 1997– .

RECORDS: NCAA all-time leader in rebounds (1,286) and blocks (396).

HONORS: Big East Player of the Year, 1994–1995; Final Four MVP, 1995; Academic All-America Player of the Year, 1995; NCAA Player of the Year, 1995; Olympic gold medalist, 1996.

Rebecca Lobo is well-liked by women's basketball fans. Despite missing almost the entire 1999 season with a knee injury, she was still voted to the All-Star team.

Rebecca Lobo
http://www.wnba.com/playerfile/rebecca_lobo.html

ANN MEYERS

ANN MEYERS BRACED HERSELF for a collision. She planted her feet in the lane and—wham!—was knocked to the hardwood floor by Indiana Pacers veteran John Kuester. The referee blew the whistle—a charging foul on Kuester. What was Meyers doing on the court with the Pacers? She was trying to make their team, of course.

Meyers had a lot of "firsts" in her career. She was the first high school player to make the U.S. National Team, the first woman to receive a full athletic scholarship to UCLA, the first four-time college All-America, and a member of the first women's Olympic team. So why not try to be the first woman in the NBA?

Meyers did not make the 1979 Pacers team. At five-feet nine-inches, she struggled against the taller players. "If she were six inches taller and forty pounds heavier, it would have been a different story," said Pacers coach Bob Leonard. "Ann did a great job from a fundamental standpoint of knowing the game of basketball. I wish some guys out there were as fundamentally sound as her."[1]

Ann Meyers was born March 26, 1955, in San Diego, California. She grew up in Orange County during a time when organized sports for girls was limited. Ann played mostly against boys until she reached high school. She then joined the girls basketball team and gained fame as a "court magician" because some of her moves seemed almost impossible. Named MVP of several area tournaments, UCLA Hall of Fame coach Billie Moore offered her a full scholarship.

Meyers proved she deserved it. As a freshman, she led the Bruins in nearly every individual category. She so

ANN MEYERS

Ann Meyers played her college ball for the UCLA Bruins. She was a four-time All-America, and was the first woman to be given the opportunity to try out for a professional men's team.

dominated the court that she led the team all four years in blocked shots, rebounds, steals, and assists. She also starred for UCLA in volleyball in the fall, and track in the spring. She became the first athlete, male or female, to be honored as a basketball All-America all four years.

In a game against Stephen F. Austin University during her senior year, Meyers became the only UCLA player in history to post a quadruple-double, reaching double figures in four statistical categories. She scored 20 points, grabbed 14 rebounds, dished out 10 assists, and made 10 steals. She capped her brilliant college career by winning the 1978 national championship. She won the Broderick Cup, given to the nation's outstanding woman athlete. Later she was named to the UCLA Hall of Fame and became the first woman to have her jersey number (fifteen) retired.

Meyers was playing for the amateur traveling team Anna's Bananas when Indiana Pacers owner Sam Nassi called out of the blue and signed Meyers to a fifty-thousand dollar personal services contract that included a possible spot on the roster. Meyers missed the cut, but at least she tried. "I did not want to look back and wonder, 'What if?'" she said. "My main purpose was to go in as a ballplayer, to hold my head up and do my best."[2]

Meyers stayed in Indiana to work for the Pacers—as an announcer. She announced Pacers games on the radio, becoming the NBA's first woman announcer—another first.

The WBL debuted in 1979, and Meyers was the first player drafted, of course. She starred for the New Jersey Gems, and was league MVP. But the WBL folded and she resumed her broadcasting career. In 1986, she married pitching great Don Drysdale, and together they became the first Hall of Fame husband and wife. In 1993, Drysdale died of a heart attack, leaving Ann a single mother of three children. Today she is an announcer for WNBA games.

ANN MEYERS

Born: March 26, 1955, San Diego, California.

High School: Sonora High School, La Habra, California, 1971, 1973–1974; Cornelia Connelly High School, Anaheim, California, 1972.

College: UCLA.

Pro: New Jersey Gems, 1979–1980.

Records: Holds UCLA career record for steals and assists, 1975–1978.

Honors: High school All-America, 1971–1974; college All-America, 1975–1978; elected to Naismith Memorial Basketball Hall of Fame, 1993.

Since ending her basketball career, Meyers has worked as an announcer and commentator for ESPN and for WNBA games.

Ann Meyers
http://espn.go.com/espninc/personalities/annmeyers.html

CHERYL MILLER

THE STREAK WAS ALIVE. USC had never lost a women's basketball game to the Arizona Wildcats. Cheryl Miller intended to keep it that way. Miller was the sharpshooter on USC's 1985 squad, and she planned to take dead aim at the basket at Arizona's McKale Center.

Miller opened the scoring with a layup. Next she hit a jumper in the lane. The Wildcats responded with baskets of their own, but Miller did not let up. The Trojans trailed by three points at halftime, but Miller kept on drilling baskets, and the Wildcats could do nothing to stop her. USC took the lead down the stretch, and Miller hit a string of free throws to hold it. When it was over, USC had won, 70–62, to extend the winning streak to 13–0.

Earlier in the year, Miller had scored 40 points to set the USC single-game record. A week later she scored 43 to break her own record. This time, against the Wildcats, she made 12 baskets and 21 free throws to finish with 45 points—to break her own record again. That mark has carried into the twenty-first century.

Cheryl Miller was born January 3, 1964, in Riverside, California. She grew up in an athletic family that strived for success. Cheryl's older brother, Darrell, became a baseball player for the California Angels and New York Yankees. Her younger brother, Reggie, is a superstar shooting guard for the Indiana Pacers. So no one who knew the Millers was surprised to see Cheryl excel at sports, even the day she scored a national record 105 points for Riverside Poly High in a 1982 contest against Norte Vista High. That senior season she was named to the high school All-America team for

Many consider Cheryl Miller to be the greatest women's basketball player of all-time.

the fourth straight year—becoming the first boy or girl so honored. She kept that streak intact at the collegiate level, achieving All-America status all four years at USC.

Miller's acrobatic play lifted the Trojans to back-to-back national titles her first two years there. A few months later she led the U.S. Women's National Team to its first Olympic gold medal. Widely considered the greatest female basketball player alive, Miller was a terror on the court but friendly and easygoing off it. Miller and her Olympic teammates often played practical jokes on one another, like the time her teammates crept into her room while she was asleep. "We put on raincoats and covered our heads," said Cynthia Cooper. "We each had a candle. We surrounded her bed and started humming. When she woke up, she was scared out of her wits. It was great!"[1]

After her playing days, Miller returned to USC as coach and guided the Trojans to their first conference title in five years. Later she worked as a television sports announcer and became active in community service work. In 1995, she became the youngest athlete ever to be enshrined in the Naismith Memorial Basketball Hall of Fame.

The creation of the WNBA in 1997 came at the perfect time for Miller, who said, "I really missed being involved in the game on the court."[2] She became the coach and general manager of the Phoenix Mercury. The following year she coached the Mercury to the WNBA Finals.

CHERYL MILLER

BORN: January 3, 1964, Riverside, California.

HIGH SCHOOL: Riverside Polytechnic High School, Riverside, California.

COLLEGE: University of Southern California.

PRO: Phoenix Mercury (coach), 1997– .

RECORDS: Scored a national record 105 points in a high school game, 1982; set numerous USC career records, including most points, rebounds, field goals, free throws, and steals.

HONORS: High school All-America, 1979–1982; member of NCAA national championship team, 1983–1984; NCAA All-America, 1983–1986; NCAA Player of the Year, 1984–1986; Olympic gold medalist, 1984; first college woman nominated for Sullivan Award (outstanding amateur athlete), 1986; elected to Naismith Memorial Basketball Hall of Fame, 1995.

Miller has worked as an announcer for both men's and women's basketball games. In 1997, she took on a new challenge as general manager and head coach of the Phoenix Mercury.

Cheryl Miller
http://www.wnba.com/mercury/coach.html

Dawn Staley

DAWN STALEY STANDS JUST FIVE FEET SIX INCHES. She is small by pro basketball standards. But Staley is the tallest basketball player in Philadelphia history in another way. On the wall of a building in downtown Philadelphia, Pennsylvania, is a mural of Staley that is over sixty feet tall.

When Staley walks past the mural at Eighth Street and Market Street, near her childhood neighborhood, she shakes her head in amazement. "You don't dream of things like that," she says. "You dream of being a part of a women's professional league in the States. You dream about becoming an Olympian and winning a gold medal. But you don't dream of having yourself on a six-story mural."[1]

Dawn Staley has worked hard to see her dreams come true. She was born May 4, 1970, in Philadelphia. She grew up in the Raymond Rosen housing project, where she showed an early love—and talent—for sports. "I didn't just play basketball," she said. "I played football, I played baseball, softball. Anything the guys were doing, I was doing."[2]

The boys and men at the Moylan Recreation Center teased Staley and told her that girls do not belong on the basketball court. Reluctantly, they let her play. Every time she got knocked down, she bounced back up. She patterned her play after Philadelphia 76ers guard Maurice Cheeks, and quickly earned respect with her scrappy style.

Dawn Staley became a starter at Dobbins Tech High School her sophomore year, and instantly jump-started the team's offense with her fancy passes and super moves. A year later she was being flooded with college scholarship offers. As a senior, she was named the National Player of

Dawn Staley of the Charlotte Sting muscles her way past the defender to get to the hoop.

the Year by *USA Today*, the first time the newspaper had ever chosen a player under six feet tall.

Dawn's mother, Estelle, and father, Clarence, had always insisted that their children work hard in school. Dawn's good grades gave her the choice of the finest universities. She picked the University of Virginia mainly for its academics. The Cavaliers did not have a winning women's basketball program, but Staley soon changed that. In her four years, she led the Cavs to a stellar 110–21 mark and three straight Final Four appearances. In the process she set dozens of records and in 1991 was awarded the Broderick Cup as the best woman athlete of any sport.

Without a pro league in the United States, Staley played the next four years overseas in countries such as Italy, France, Spain, and Brazil. During this stretch she often returned to the United States for two reasons—to play for the national team, and to check into the hospital. Staley had suffered from chronic knee problems since college. She has had so many surgeries on her knees that she has lost count.

Staley realized her ultimate dream in 1996 when she helped the United States win the Olympic gold medal. She was so excited to hear the final buzzer sound in the title game that she did cartwheels across the court. And then another dream came true. A professional league in her own country was starting. Staley signed up for the American Basketball League (ABL) and joined the Richmond Rage, where she put her magic on display. A year later, the Rage relocated to Philadelphia. Staley was called "The Lady Magic Johnson" by the NBA showman himself, who said, "She's a show-stopper. She's what it's all about—no-look, behind-the-back, behind-the-legs."[3] Staley is playing her stylish game in the WNBA now, where she wears a rubber band on her right wrist. When she makes a mistake, she snaps the rubber band. She does not snap it often.

DAWN STALEY

BORN: May 4, 1970, Philadelphia, Pennsylvania.

HIGH SCHOOL: Dobbins Tech High School, Philadelphia, Pennsylvania.

COLLEGE: University of Virginia.

PRO: Played on various teams in France, Italy, Spain, and Brazil, 1992–1995; Philadelphia Rage (ABL), 1996–1998; Charlotte Sting (WNBA), 1999– .

RECORDS: NCAA all-time leader in steals; Atlantic Coast Conference all-time leader in assists.

HONORS: NCAA All-America, 1990–1992; NCAA Player of the Year, 1991–1992; USA Basketball Female Athlete of the Year, 1994; Olympic gold medalist, 1996; American Basketball League First-Team, 1997.

Sprinting to the basket, Dawn Staley looks to beat the other team down the floor. Staley grew up in a poor section of Philadelphia, but did not let that distract her from reaching her goals.

Dawn Staley
http://www.wnba.com/playerfile/dawn_staley.html

SHERYL SWOOPES

The defender can only watch as Sheryl Swoopes beats her to the basket for the easy finger-roll.

SHERYL SWOOPES WAS IN THE ZONE. It seemed as if the players around her were moving in slow motion. Her own shooting motion felt effortless. It was like a dream. "At times, I get it in my mind that there is no way I can miss," said Swoopes.[1] This was one of those times.

It was the 1993 NCAA Women's Basketball Championship between the Ohio State Buckeyes and Texas Tech Red Raiders. Ohio State had two cat-quick guards and three tenacious frontcourt players. Texas Tech had Sheryl Swoopes. The Buckeyes employed several defenses to try to contain Swoopes, sometimes rotating defenders, sometimes triple-teaming her. But as Ohio State head coach Nancy Darsch said, "She answered everything we tried. You don't appreciate Sheryl Swoopes until you have to stop her."[2]

The Red Raiders won the game, 84–82. "When it was over," Swoopes said, "my first thought was, 'Is this real?'"[3] Swoopes scored 47 points against the Buckeyes—the most points ever scored in a college championship game. The previous women's record was 28, while the men's mark was 44, set by UCLA's Bill Walton twenty years earlier. Swoopes broke nine other records in the tournament, further cementing her reputation as "the female Michael Jordan."

Sheryl Swoopes was born March 25, 1971, in Brownfield, Texas. She learned to play basketball against her three brothers, and by age eight led a team called the Little Dribblers to a national tournament. She guided Brownfield High School to three state titles and earned a scholarship to the University of Texas. But the college was four hundred miles away, and Swoopes immediately got homesick. She returned to Brownfield three days later. She enrolled at a local junior college and became the National Junior College Player of the Year.

As a junior, Swoopes enrolled at nearby Texas Tech. The Red Raiders had never won an NCAA tournament game, but Swoopes single-handedly turned the program into a national power. With her dynamic moves, she averaged nearly 22 points a game, and became known as the "Texas Tornado." The comparisons to NBA great Michael Jordan soon followed.

Swoopes played briefly in the European League before returning home to work at a bank. Her fame soared soon after when she made the U.S. Women's National Team and won medals at such international competitions as the 1994 World Championships in Australia and Goodwill Games in Russia. She played the great Jordan in a one-on-one game and held her own, losing 7–5. She then became the first woman athlete ever to have a shoe named after her—the Nike Air Swoopes. She capped her amateur career by leading the United States to the gold medal at the 1996 Olympic Games.

Sheryl Swoopes was supposed to be a marquee name for the WNBA. Instead, four days before the league's 1997 debut, she was in a hospital giving birth. She named her son Jordan. Then, forty-three days later, she was back on the court as a starting forward for the Houston Comets. "I hope that my decision to have a child and return to basketball will serve as an inspiration to working mothers everywhere," she said.[4] Together with Cynthia Cooper, she led the Comets to the WNBA title. And just as Michael Jordan did with the Chicago Bulls, Swoopes built her team into a dynasty, leading it to the next two league titles as well, and giving the WNBA its first "three-peat" champion.

BORN: March 25, 1971, Brownfield, Texas.

HIGH SCHOOL: Brownfield High School, Brownfield, Texas.

COLLEGE: Texas Tech University.

PRO: European League, 1993; Houston Comets, 1997– .

RECORDS: NCAA Championship Game scoring record (47 points), 1993; recorded WNBA's first triple-double (14 points, 15 rebounds, 10 assists), 1999.

HONORS: Texas high school Player of the Year, 1989; NCAA Final Four MVP, 1993; NCAA Player of the Year, 1993; Olympic gold medalist, 1996.

Looking to make a play, Sheryl Swoopes dribbles through a crowd of defenders. In 1997, Swoopes took time out of her basketball career to have a baby. Roughly a month-and-a-half after her son was born, she was back on the court.

Sheryl Swoopes
http://www.wnba.com/playerfile/sheryl_swoopes.html

CHAPTER NOTES

Introduction

1. Mary Duffy, "Center of Attention," *Women's Sports & Fitness*, March 1996, p. 70.

Cynthia Cooper

1. Staff, "Three-Peat," *WNBA.com*, September 9, 1999, <http://www.wnba.com/championship99/990905/nylhou/recap.html> (May 11, 2000).

2. Ibid.

3. Richard Hoffer, "Family Ties," *Sports Illustrated for Women*, Summer 1999, p. 93.

4. Staff, "Ask the Athletes," *Sports Illustrated for Kids*, July 1999, p. 13.

5. Judith Graham, ed., *Current Biography Yearbook* (New York: H. W. Wilson Company, 1998), p. 128.

6. Hoffer, p. 94.

Anne Donovan

1. AP Staff, "Donovan Showed Character," *Newport News-Daily Press*, September 30, 1988, p. 1.

Chamique Holdsclaw

1. Michelle R. Derrow, "Spotlight," *Time for Kids*, March 5, 1999, p. 8.

2. Ibid.

3. James Ponti, *WNBA: Stars of Women's Basketball* (New York: Simon & Schuster, 1999), pp. 10–11.

Lisa Leslie

1. Staff, "West All-Stars 79, East All-Stars 61," *WNBA.com*, July 14, 1999, <http://www.wnba.com/games99/990714/weseas/recap.html> (May 11, 2000).

2. Ibid.

3. Molly Jackel, *Fast Breaks—WNBA Superstars* (New York: Scholastic, Inc., 1998), p. 31.

Nancy Lieberman-Cline

1. John Riha, "On the Ball," *World Traveler*, August 1998, p. 38.

2. Ibid, p. 36.

3. Bill Gutman, *Shooting Stars: The Women of Pro Basketball* (New York: Random House, 1998), p. 28.

Rebecca Lobo

1. Staff, "The Worst Day I Ever Had," *Sports Illustrated for Kids*, June 1995, p. 51.

2. Barbara Jones, "Courage That Runs in the Family," *Good Housekeeping*, May 1996, p. 22.

3. Ruth Ann & Rebecca Lobo, *The Home Team* (New York: Kodansha America, Inc., 1996), p. 7.

4. Marty Kaminsky, "Playing For Liberty," *Highlights for Children*, May 1999, p. 23.

5. Ibid.

Ann Meyers

1. Bill Gutman, *Shooting Stars: The Women of Pro Basketball* (New York: Random House, 1998), pp. 25–26.

2. Ibid, p. 26.

Cheryl Miller

1. Staff, "Ask the Athletes," *Sports Illustrated for Kids*, April 1998, p. 13.

2. Bob Cunningham, "Just Call Her Coach!" *Inland Empire*, June 1998, p. 57.

Dawn Staley

1. Kristi Nelson, "Dawn of a New Era," *Hoop Magazine*, February 1999, p. 13.

2. Ibid.

3. Rachel Rutledge, *The Best of the Best in Basketball* (Brookfield, Conn.: The Millbrook Press, 1998), p. 48.

Sheryl Swoopes

1. Judith Graham, *Current Biography Yearbook* (New York: H.W. Wilson Company, 1996), p. 559.

2. Ibid, p. 560.

3. Ibid, p. 559.

4. Rachel Rutledge, *The Best of the Best in Basketball* (Brookfield, Conn.: The Millbrook Press, 1998), p. 61.

INDEX